PRESENTED TO:

_____

FROM:

_____

DATE:

_____

Jesus calling®

FOR TEENS

50 DEVOTIONS FOR A THANKFUL HEART

Sarah Young

Adapted by Tama Fortner

Edited by Kris Bearss

THOMAS NELSON
Since 1798

Published in Nashville, Tennessee, by Tommy Nelson. Tommy Nelson is an imprint of Thomas Nelson. Thomas Nelson is a registered trademark of HarperCollins Christian Publishing, Inc.

Unless otherwise noted, Scripture quotations used in this book are from: The Holy Bible, New International Version®. © 1973, 1978, 1984 by Biblica, Inc.™ Used by permission of Zondervan. All rights reserved worldwide. www.zondervan.com. The "NIV"and "New International Version" are trademarks registered in the United States Patent and Trademark Office by Biblica, Inc.™

Scripture quotations marked CEV are taken from the Contemporary English Version®, © 1995 American Bible Society. All rights reserved.

Scripture quotations marked ICB are taken from the International Children's Bible®. Copyright © 1986, 1988, 1999 by Thomas Nelson. Used by permission. All rights reserved.

Scripture quotations marked NKJV are taken from the New King James Version. © 1982 by Thomas Nelson. Used by permission. All rights reserved.

Scripture quotations marked NLT are taken the Holy Bible, New Living Translation © copyright 1996, 2004 by Tyndale House Foundation. Used by permission of Tyndale House Publishers, Inc., Carol Stream, Illinois 60188. All rights reserved.

ISBN 978-1-4003-2436-1

Library of Congress Cataloging-in-Publication Data

Fortner, Tama, 1969–
Jesus calling: 365 devotions for kids / Sarah Young; adapted by Tama Fortner; edited by Kris Bearss.
p. cm.
ISBN 978–1–4003–1634–2 (hardcover)
1. Devotional calendars—Juvenile literature. I. Young, Sarah, 1946–II. Bearss, Kris. III. Young, Sarah, 1946–Jesus calling. IV. Title.
BV4870.F67 2010
242'.62—dc22   2010017099

Printed in China

18 19 20 21 22 DSC 5 4 3 2 1

INTRODUCTION

When we come to Jesus with a thankful heart, we can set aside worries and enjoy His presence. This grateful attitude helps us focus on our blessings and look for the miracles Jesus weaves into our lives.

Through gratitude, the Word of Christ can live in us (Colossians 3:16). This is important because the Bible is the only perfect Word of God—without errors. As you spend time in the Word and in this devotional, be assured that I work hard to keep my writings consistent with the unchanging truths of Scripture.

I have written from the perspective of Jesus speaking, to help readers feel more personally connected with Him. So the first person singular ("I," "Me," "My," "Mine") always refers to Jesus; "you" refers to you, the reader. I've included Scripture references after each reading. Words from the Bible (some paraphrased, some quoted) are written in italics.

"Give thanks in all circumstances, for this is God's will for you in Christ Jesus" (1 Thessalonians 5:18).

Sarah Young

I LOVE THAT!

It is not possible to thank Me too much. I love your praises. Sometimes your praise is an unplanned, in-the-moment, you-just-can't-help-yourself sort of thing. Perhaps you have just received one of My blessings or have been overwhelmed by the beauty of My creation, and you are just bursting to tell Me about it. I love that!

Other times, you stop to think about My blessings, about My Presence in your life. And you decide to thank Me. I love that kind of praise too.

When you are struggling with a problem, pray about it. Then go ahead and thank Me for the help you know I will give you. This kind of praise means you know I am in control—and I love that!

Fill up the spare moments of your life with praise, and you will find that your life is filled with Me.

PSALM 22:3; PSALM 146:1–2

Give THANKS

whatever happens.

That is what

God WANTS

for you in

Christ Jesus.

—1 THESSALONIANS 5:18 (ICB)

EXPECT SURPRISES!

Try to see each day as an adventure, planned out by Me, your Guide. Instead of trying to make your day into what you want it to be, open your eyes to all the things I have prepared just for you. Each day is My precious gift to you—and you only have one chance to live it. Trust that I am with you every minute, working in your life. And then thank Me for this day—no matter what happens.

Expect surprises! When you live your life with Me, no day will ever be boring or predictable. Don't take the easiest path. Don't just get through the day. Live it! Be willing to follow Me wherever I lead. Even when My way seems scary, the safest place to be is by My side.

1 PETER 2:21

This is the DAY

the Lord has made;

let us REJOICE

and be GLAD in it.

—Psalm 118:24

NO MORE BORING DAYS

Come to Me with a thankful heart. I have made this day for you so that you can enjoy My Presence in it. Don't worry about tomorrow. Rejoice in today. Look for the many blessings and miracles that I have put into this day. If you look for My Presence in your life, you will find it.

Come to Me with all your needs, big and small, knowing that I will take care of you. When you are not worried about what is happening in your life, then you are free to truly live. I want to give you that freedom. Turn your heart over to Me and I will fill it with peace and joy. And there will be no more boring days!

PSALM 118:24; PHILIPPIANS 4:19

Do not worry about anything. But PRAY and ask God for everything you need. And when you pray, always give THANKS. And God's peace will keep your hearts and minds in Christ Jesus. The PEACE that God gives is so great that we cannot understand it.

—Philippians 4:6–7 (ICB)

NO MORE COMPARISONS

I know that sometimes you doubt yourself. You worry what people think about you. You are afraid that you're not good enough. You think no one cares.

I want you to bring those fears and doubts to Me and let Me give you peace. Accept yourself as the person I created you to be. Don't wear yourself out comparing yourself to others. Instead, be thankful for how I made you, and trust Me as I guide you through this day.

As you learn to live with Me as the Center of your life, My Peace will fill you up. You will stop worrying about how you look and what other people think of you, because you will be too busy living the life I have planned for you.

PSALM 29:11; NUMBERS 6:24−25; PSALM 13:5

May the Lord

WATCH over

you and

GIVE

you peace.

—Numbers 6:26 (icb)

STILL AND QUIET

It's tough to be still and quiet. There are so many things you could be doing—playing outside, talking to a friend, going to the game. But there are times when you have to be still—when you are sick, when you have finished your classwork, or when others need you to be quiet. Instead of wishing away this time, use it to listen for Me and to thank Me for My Presence in your life.

Some of My greatest work is done when you are still and quiet. That is when you can hear Me whisper to your heart.

ISAIAH 30:15; 2 CORINTHIANS 12:9

"Be

STILL

before

the

LORD."

—ZECHARIAH 2:13

Let them give thanks
to the LORD for his
unfailing love and his
wonderful deeds for men.

—Psalm 107:8

IT'S YOUR CHOICE

rust and *thankfulness*. You hear those words a lot, but why are they so important to Me? Because they are the two things that you must have to stay close to Me.

When you *trust* Me, you are not worrying or trying to fix things yourself. You are keeping your eyes on Me, thinking about Me and what I want for you. When you are *thankful* to Me, there is no room for criticizing or complaining—those sins that can trip you up by tearing down other people.

Trusting and being thankful are choices that only you can make. And you'll have to make them every single day, many times a day. Just as with sports or math or any other skill, the more you practice, the easier it becomes!

PSALM 141:8; 1 PETER 5:7

As you RECEIVED Christ Jesus the Lord, so continue to live in him. Keep your roots deep in him and have your lives BUILT on him. Be strong in the faith, just as you were taught. And always be THANKFUL.

—COLOSSIANS 2:6–7 (ICB)

SLOW DOWN!

The alarm clock goes off and you bolt out of bed like a racehorse. You dash to the kitchen, wolf down some breakfast, and then it's out the door. You run, run, run through your day . . .

Slow down! Did you yawn and stretch and thank Me for a healthy body that can get out of bed? Did you peek outside and see that beautiful sunrise I made for you? Did you thank Me for the food you ate? Or the home you live in? Or the people who love you?

Don't be so rushed that you forget to notice the blessings I fill your day with. Stop for a moment. Enjoy. Thank Me. Thankfulness not only pleases Me, but it also protects you from thoughts that make you sad. When you're thankful for the blessings all around you, you feel much happier. So slow down—and give thanks!

1 THESSALONIANS 5:18 (ICB)

Continue

PRAYING

and keep alert.

And when you pray,

always THANK God.

—Colossians 4:2 (icb)

THE GIFT OF THE SPIRIT

I shower blessings down on you every day. Even when you don't notice them, they are there.

One of my greatest blessings is the gift of the Holy Spirit. He lives within you, teaching and guiding you.

The Holy Spirit is like a great multiplier. In math, five plus five equals ten. But five *times* five equals twenty-five—a much bigger result. The Holy Spirit works in much the same way. He takes your faith and multiplies it. You may start with a small bit of faith in Me, but the Spirit works to multiply it so that it grows much greater.

Be sure to thank Me for the gift of My Spirit. This helps Him to work more freely in you, making you even *more* thankful—and more joyful too!

2 CORINTHIANS 3:17; PSALM 50:14

This is what

God MADE us for.

And he has given us

the Spirit to be a

guarantee for

this NEW life.

—2 Corinthians 5:5 (icb)

A JOYFUL HEART

Rejoice! To rejoice in Me is to praise Me with joy and thankfulness. I love to hear you rejoicing. You can sing it. You can shout it. You can whisper it softly—or even pray silently. It doesn't matter *how* you do it; it matters only *that* you do it! Make this a new habit in your life.

When you rejoice in Me, I am lifted up—and I lift you up as well. Rejoicing tells Me that you know your blessings come from Me, and this makes Me want to bless you even more. I do My greatest works through people who have joyful, thankful hearts. So rejoice in Me always. In every situation. As you practice this habit of praise, your life will get better and better!

PSALM 95:1–2; PSALM 9:10

REJOICE

in the Lord

ALWAYS.

I will say it

again: Rejoice!

—Philippians 4:4

NO GRUMBLING, PLEASE

Grumbling and complaining are not what I want from you. When you grumble, you are telling Me that you don't like the way things are going in your life—that you hate My way of doing things. And when you complain, you are showing an ungrateful heart.

Thankfulness is your protection against the sins of grumbling and complaining. Being thankful also keeps you close to Me. So—when you have too much homework, when your parents give you an extra chore, or when I've said "not now" to one of your prayers—don't grumble or mumble under your breath. Instead, *thank Me* for the things that upset you. Before you know it, you will start to see those things differently. And you'll start to feel better too.

1 CORINTHIANS 10:10; HEBREWS 12:28–29;
1 THESSALONIANS 5:18

And

DO NOT

grumble.

—1 Corinthians 10:10

Through Jesus, therefore, let us continually offer to God a sacrifice of praise—the fruit of lips that confess his name.

—Hebrews 13:15

OPEN YOUR EYES

I want your *sacrifice* of thanksgiving. But what does that mean? It means that I want you to put aside your favorite show, your MP3 player, your free time—and choose Me instead. I want you to put aside what you want for yourself for a while so that you can spend time with Me.

A sacrifice of *thanksgiving* also means that you are thankful, *no matter what*. If you choose to see only what is wrong, or what is making you unhappy, then your mind will be filled with dark thoughts. If you refuse to enjoy life until that problem is "fixed," you will miss out on My daily blessings of sunshine, flowers, friends—of life and salvation.

Come to Me with a thankful heart—always! Yes, even when something is wrong. Let My Light open your eyes to see the blessings I pour out upon you—day after day after day.

GENESIS 3:2–6; 1 JOHN 1:7

I will **OFFER**

you a sacrifice

to show how

GRATEFUL I am,

and I will pray.

—PSALM 116:17 (CEV)

JUST TODAY

I have made this day for you. Be careful not to complain about anything in it—not your English test, not your frizzy hair, not even the weather—because I am the Creator of this day. Instead, *decide* to be happy today. Open your eyes, and choose to look for all the blessings I have hidden in this day.

Then live today—*just today*. Don't think about mistakes you've made in the past. Don't worry about what will happen tomorrow. You will only end up wasting today. I want you to enjoy abundant Life in My Presence—today!

PSALM 118:24

Forgetting what is behind

and straining TOWARD what

is ahead, I press on toward

the GOAL to win the prize

for which God has called me

HEAVENWARD in Christ Jesus.

—PHILIPPIANS 3:13–14

EVEN WHEN YOU DON'T UNDERSTAND

Every day, every minute, every second, I want you to be filled with thankfulness—not with complaining. I am the Creator and the Controller of all the universe. Heaven and earth are filled with My Glory.

When you complain, you are saying that you think you could run the world better than I do. Things will happen that you don't understand. You ask "why?" and "why not?" But you do not know all the things that I know. You can only see today. I can see yesterday, today, and forever—all at the same time. I know how everything fits together.

Have faith in Me and trust that I will take care of you. Be thankful and praise Me—even when you don't understand.

HEBREWS 13:8; 2 CORINTHIANS 5:7;
1 THESSALONIANS 5:18

And they were

CALLING to

one another:

"Holy, holy, holy

is the Lord ALMIGHTY;

the whole earth is

full of his GLORY."

—ISAIAH 6:3

SO MANY BLESSINGS

Let Me teach you how to be thankful. First, think about all the things you have to be thankful for—home, family, friends, food, clothes, stuff. Then, think about how each of these things is a gift from Me.

As the sun rises, remember that today is a gift from Me. As you get out of bed, think about the gift of a healthy body. As you gather up your schoolwork and prepare for the day, be grateful for your abilities and talents. Try to count the many good things I have filled your life with. Is it twenty-five? Fifty? One hundred? I dare you to try to count all My blessings.

The secret to being thankful is thinking about all the good things in your life—and then remembering that these are all gifts from Me.

HEBREWS 12:29; PSALM 119:105

Therefore,

since we are

RECEIVING

a kingdom that

cannot be shaken,

let us be THANKFUL.

—HEBREWS 12:28

I AM GOOD

I am good. I am not just good one day and then not-so-good the next. I am *always* good. I will always do what is good and best for you.

And I am *completely* good. Not just mostly good, or 99.9 percent good. I am Light, and there is no darkness in Me—none at all!

So come to Me with a thankful heart. Be glad that your life is not at the whim of an imperfect God. Be grateful that you serve a perfect God who wants only the very best for you. Expect Me to take care of you. There is not a single thing you need that I cannot give you.

1 JOHN 1:5

Let us come

before him with

THANKSGIVING

and extol him with

music and song.

—Psalm 95:2

But let all who take refuge in you be glad; let them ever sing for joy. Spread your protection over them, that those who love your name may rejoice in you.

—Psalm 5:11

DON'T BORROW WORRIES

Whenever your mind gets stuck on a problem, bring it to Me and thank Me for it. Ask Me to show you My way of handling it. When you do this, your mind is freed and the problem is robbed of its power to make you worry. Together, we will deal with your problem, either facing it right now or putting it aside for later.

You see, many of the worries that tangle up your mind today are actually ones that you have borrowed from tomorrow. Don't waste time worrying about whether or not you will make the team next year, or pass the class next semester, or even what you will do this weekend. Give those borrowed worries to Me and let Me put them in the future where they belong. Leave them there—out of sight—and I will replace them with My Peace.

PHILIPPIANS 4:6

"**PEACE** I leave

with you;

my peace

I **GIVE** you."

—John 14:27

JUST WHAT YOU NEED

I am Immanuel. My Name means *God with you*. And that is who I am. I am God, and I am always with you, constantly watching over you. You are surrounded by My Love and My Presence. There is nothing that can ever separate you from Me—not even the worst of troubles.

Some people feel closest to Me during happy times, when they can see My blessings and sing My praises. Others feel closest to Me in times of trouble—when their trust in Me helps them feel My hand leading them to safety. But both the troubles and the joys are My gifts to you.

Each day I provide just what you need, to draw you closer to Me. Try to see everything that happens as My gift designed just for you. This helps you to be thankful—even in times of trouble.

COLOSSIANS 2:6–7

"They will

call him

IMMANUEL"—

which means,

"God with us."

—Matthew 1:23

WHEN YOU
ARE AFRAID . . .

I want to be the Center of your life. When you focus on Me, My Peace chases away your fears and worries.

I know . . . *everyone* is afraid sometimes. I am not saying that you will *never* be afraid. What I am saying is that you never have to face your fears alone. I am *always* with you, and My Strength is *always* there for you. I will *never* leave you.

But fear is a sneaky thing. Just when you think you've gotten it out of your life, it will creep up behind and whisper in your ear: *You're all alone.* But remember My words: *I am always with you.*

Thank Me for My Presence, and trust Me; this will protect you from fear. Spend time in the Light of My Love, while I bless you with My Peace.

2 THESSALONIANS 3:16

Where God's

LOVE is, there

is no fear,

because God's

PERFECT love

takes away fear.

—1 JOHN 4:18 (ICB)

WORTH CELEBRATING

Consider problems as pure joy. That's not the way the world usually looks at problems, is it? The world says to do everything you can to *avoid* problems. But there is simply no way to avoid every problem, no matter how hard you try.

The best way to get through a difficult day is to hold My hand tightly and keep talking to Me. As we talk, be sure to tell Me you trust Me—and thank Me for My help. Ask Me to guide you through your problems and show you the blessings hidden in them.

The blessing of self-control can be learned from dealing with a difficult teacher. The blessing of patience can be learned from an illness. I teach you many things through your problems. I also use them to draw you closer to Me.

So yes, consider problems as pure joy, knowing that with Me by your side, they can become things worth celebrating.

PHILIPPIANS 4:13; ISAIAH 26:3

Consider it pure JOY,

my brothers,

whenever you

face TRIALS of

many kinds.

—James 1:2

YOUR BEST PROTECTION

I am always near. So I know that sometimes you get angry at Me—and may even feel like shaking your fist in My Face. You are tempted to complain about the way I am treating you. You want to rebel against Me. But that is a dangerous thing to do. Once you step over that line, rivers of rage and self-pity can sweep you away.

Your best protection is to thank Me for the things that are troubling you. You see, it is impossible for you to thank Me and complain at the same time. It may feel weird at first to thank Me when you are upset with Me. But keep trying. Your thankful words, prayed in faith, will change your heart and bring you closer to Me.

PSALM 116:17; PHILIPPIANS 4:4, 6

The

LORD

is **NEAR.**

—Philippians 4:5

Always giving thanks to God the Father for everything, in the name of our Lord Jesus Christ.

—Ephesians 5:20

YOU MAKE ME SING!

When you make a special gift for someone, you can't wait to see that person open it. That smile, that hug, those words of thanks just feel so good!

I am the same way. I want you to begin each day by opening up your hands and your heart to receive My gifts. From the morning sunrise to the evening stars, I have prepared so many gifts for you. And I can't wait to see what you think of each one. Will you notice that flower I planted along your path? Will you see that cloud I shaped for you? Will you remember to thank Me?

When you praise Me for the gifts I have made, you open up your heart to Me. Your smiles, your songs, your words of praise just feel so good! Remember that I take great joy in you—you make Me sing!

PSALM 118:24; PSALM 95:2

He will

REJOICE

over you with

SINGING.

—Zephaniah 3:17

SINGING WITH THE ANGELS

You've heard people say things like, "She sings like an angel." But did you know that you really can sing *with* the angels? When you worship Me in spirit and truth, your voice joins with choirs of angels who are always praising Me. While you can't hear their voices, I hear every word of your worship and praise.

To worship in spirit and in truth means that you truly *worship* Me. You don't just go through the motions—sitting and standing at the right times, closing your eyes to pray. It means that your heart and your spirit are really praising Me, because you know I am the All-Powerful God.

When you truly worship Me, it opens the way to My Heart. Then My blessings rain down on you. And the greatest blessing of all is simply being *near* Me.

JOHN 4:23; PSALM 100:4

"God is spirit,

and his

WORSHIPERS

must worship

in spirit and in

TRUTH."

—JOHN 4:24

BE THANKFUL

I am always with you. But I have given you the freedom to choose whether or not you want to be close to Me. I want you to come to Me because you love Me, not because you have to. So I have placed a "door" between us, and I let you decide whether or not to open it.

One of the best ways to open that door is to *be thankful*. I especially want you to learn to thank Me when times are tough. Your thankfulness tells Me that you trust Me. So when thankful words stick in your throat, check to see if you really do trust Me—even in hard times.

Try seeing how many times you can thank Me each day. This will help you see all the good things I give you—day after day. It will also help you want to *praise My Name*!

1 THESSALONIANS 5:18

Enter his gates with

THANKSGIVING and

his courts with praise;

give thanks to him and

PRAISE his name.

—PSALM 100:4

AN ADVENTURE WITH ME

Living your life while depending on Me is a great adventure. Most people—grown-ups and kids alike—scurry around trying to do things their own way. Some are huge successes; others fail miserably. But both miss out on what life is supposed to be—*an adventure with Me.*

When you give control of your life to Me, I open your eyes so that you can see Me at work in the world. Where others see "coincidences," you see My wonderful work—even miracles at times. And where others see only an everyday happening, you see Me.

Live each day just watching for what I will do next. You are in Me, and I am in you—and through Me you learn to truly live. This is the amazing adventure I offer you.

2 CORINTHIANS 12:9–10;
ACTS 17:28; COLOSSIANS 2:6–7

"On that

day you will

REALIZE that I

am in my Father,

and you are in me,

and I AM in you."

—John 14:20

CHASING AWAY THE FOG

Some mornings you wake up and the world is blanketed with a thick fog. As you look out your window, you can trace the outline of the house across the street and perhaps the car out front. But the details are impossible to see.

That is what living with worry and fear is like. They create a fog in your mind and heart that keeps you from seeing Me clearly. But just as the sunlight chases away the morning fog, My Light chases away the fog of fear and worry.

All you have to do is tell Me about your worries and fears, and then leave them with Me. Don't snatch them back again! Trust Me to help you handle everything that happens, knowing it doesn't surprise Me. And count on Me to take care of you. Let My Light chase away the fog. Then go out and live your day in the sunshine of My Love.

PSALM 118:24 (NLT); 1 THESSALONIANS 5:18

So be HUMBLE under

God's powerful hand.

Then he will LIFT you up

when the right time comes.

Give all your worries to him,

because he CARES for you.

—1 PETER 5:6–7 (ICB)

Delight yourself in the LORD
and he will give you the
desires of your heart.

—Psalm 37:4

TOUGH IT OUT

Tough it out." "Stay strong." "Endure." You hear these words a lot when people are talking about sports. But they don't sound so great when you're talking about your life. And yet, that is what you must do: Tough it out, stay strong, and endure.

It's just a fact. You are going to have troubles in this life. The devil is your enemy. So he is going to throw everything he has at you. Problems at school, home, and with friends. Fear, loneliness, and doubt. Expect these troubles, and stand strong. And when the evil one attacks, give thanks.

Yes, give thanks! Thank Me for being able to bring good out of everything. Praise Me for the chance to see My Power in your life. Worship Me—the God who always has a purpose, and who will not let the evil one snatch you away. And thank Me for the spiritual strength you gain by enduring your troubles bravely.

JAMES 1:2–4; PSALM 107:21–22

You KNOW that
you learn to
ENDURE by having
your faith tested.

—James 1:3 (cev)

TELL IT TO ME

You don't like it when your plans are messed with. You planned to go to the movies, but your parents said no. You wanted to spend the summer goofing off, but you ended up babysitting instead. You had a goal in mind, but I said, "Not now."

When you don't get to do what you want, you feel like stomping your foot and yelling, "No!" But instead, you push your anger and frustration down inside you. I want you to let that frustration out—to Me. I'll understand, and I'll help you sort through it. Then—and this is the really tough part—praise Me.

Remember that all good things—your possessions, your family and friends, your health and talents, even your time—are *gifts* from Me. Thank Me for the good things I give you, but do not cling to them. Be willing to let go of anything I take from you, including your plans. But don't ever let go of My hand!

PSALM 139:23–24; 1 PETER 5:6

The Lord GAVE

me what I had,

and the Lord has

TAKEN it away.

Praise the name

of the Lord!

—Job 1:21 (NLT)

YOU CAN'T EARN
MY BLESSINGS

This is a time of plenty in your life. Your cup over-flows with blessings. Enjoy this time—it is My gift to you.

Don't feel guilty when everything is going well. Don't turn away from My blessings because you think you don't deserve to be so blessed. That is nonsense. The truth is that no one deserves anything from Me. My kingdom is not about earning blessings. And life with Me is not some sort of game in which you earn points to buy prizes. Good behavior doesn't buy blessings.

Instead of trying to work for My blessings, I want you to receive them thankfully. I give you good gifts because I love to see your joy when you receive them. So open your hands and your heart, and accept My blessings gratefully. This brings Joy to you *and* to Me!

JOHN 3:16; LUKE 11:9–10; ROMANS 8:32

My cup

OVERFLOWS

with blessings.

—Psalm 23:5 (NLT)

WINDOWS OF HEAVEN

When you come to Me with a thankful heart, it opens up windows of heaven. Spiritual blessings fall freely through those windows and down into your life. A thankful heart opens you up to these blessings, and then you have even *more* reasons to be grateful.

Being thankful brings you many blessings, but it is not a magic formula. Thankful words are really just the language of Love, and they help you grow closer to Me. When you thank Me, it makes a love-connection between your heart and Mine. Just as a telephone connection lets you talk to another person, a loving, thankful heart helps you talk to Me—and Me to you.

Being thankful doesn't mean you close your eyes to the many problems in this world. It means you find Joy in Me—your Savior—in the midst of a messed-up world. I am your hiding place and your strength. And I'm always ready to help you!

HABAKKUK 3:17–18; PSALM 46:1

I will REJOICE

in the LORD,

I will be JOYFUL

in God my Savior.

—HABAKKUK 3:18

A BOUQUET
OF TREASURES

As you go through this day, look for the tiny treasures I have placed along your way. I lovingly go before you and plant little pleasures to brighten up your day.

Sometimes these treasures are a part of My creation—a bird hopping by, a multicolored sunset, a tiny wildflower. Other times I use people in your life to deliver My pleasures to you—an encouraging note from a teacher, a hug from a friend at just the right moment, a smile from someone you don't even know.

Collect these treasures one by one. When you reach the end of your day, you will have gathered a beautiful bouquet of them. Offer them back to Me with a thankful heart. Then receive My Peace as you lie down in your bed, letting your thankful thoughts sing you to sleep.

ROMANS 8:38–39; PSALM 4:7

I will lie down

and SLEEP in peace,

for you ALONE,

O Lord, make

me dwell in SAFETY.

—Psalm 4:8

I praise you because you made me in an amazing and wonderful way. What you have done is wonderful. I know this very well.

—Psalm 139:14 (ICB)

I AM GOOD

I *am* good. Walk with Me today and see that for yourself. The more time you spend with Me, the more you will see just how good I am. And I promise to do only what is good for you.

When hard times come, many people start to doubt My goodness. But troubles are just part of living in this imperfect world. And I can use your troubles to grow your faith.

I know that doesn't always make sense to you. You won't always understand the "why" of things. I am God, and My thoughts and My ways are incredibly bigger and more complicated than yours. When you don't understand, just *trust* that I am good—and that I *always* work for good in your life.

ISAIAH 55:8–9

Examine and

see how GOOD

the Lord is.

Happy is the

person who

TRUSTS the Lord.

—Psalm 34:8 (icb)

I DID IT FOR YOU

When I came to earth, it wasn't to a palace or a rich family. I was born to a peasant girl and a carpenter, in a stable. My Glory was hidden from all but a few people.

At times, some of My Glory would shine out of Me—especially when I began to do miracles. When the sick were healed, when the storms were stilled, and when the demons fled before Me, people saw it . . . briefly.

At the end of My life, I could have used My awesome Power to save Myself. Thousands of angels would have come to rescue Me from being beaten and made fun of and nailed to a cross. But that was not My Father's plan. So I stayed on the cross—for you. I did it so that your sins could be forgiven and heaven could become your home. I did it so that we could be the best of friends. So let your life become a song of praise to Me, showing My Glory to all the world.

JOHN 2:11; LUKE 23:36; PSALM 92:1–5

The people

STOOD watching,

and the rulers even

sneered at him. They said,

"He **SAVED** others; let him

save himself if he is the Christ

of God, the **CHOSEN** One."

—LUKE 23:35

WINNING MY WAY

What does it mean to *win*? Your friends—and maybe even some grown-ups—may say that winning means never messing up, never failing. It is being the best, better than anyone else, and being in total control. That is how this world sees winning.

But I have another definition. Winning—for all eternity—is about letting *Me* have total control. It is admitting that you need Me, and then trusting Me to lead you.

Don't just ask Me to bless what you have already decided to do. Ask Me what I want for you. I may fill your heart with a dream that seems impossibly far beyond your reach. And that dream will be bigger than anything you can do on your own. But remember, nothing is beyond *My* reach.

Yes, you will mess up sometimes, and you will make mistakes. But when you depend on Me, I will use your mistakes to grow your faith and to help you win—*My way*!

PSALM 34:17–18

But we

LIVE by faith,

not by what

we **SEE.**

—2 CORINTHIANS 5:7 (CEV)

SOMETIMES I WHISPER

I am *always* with you. Even now, I am here with you. That soft whisper in your mind? That's from Me. That gentle tap on your heart? That's from Me too. I have all the Power in heaven and on earth. With My Might, I can control the very wind and the waves, but with you I am quiet and tender. And the more you are hurting, the more tender I am.

When others leave you feeling worthless and alone, hope in Me. My hope is not just a wish for things to be better; it is My promise to you that I will always help you. I will carry your troubles for you and lighten your heart. I am your ever-present Help, so you are never alone.

ROMANS 12:12; ROMANS 15:13

God is our

REFUGE and strength,

an ever-present

HELP in trouble.

—Psalm 46:1

BE BOLD!

oday is an adventure, and I want you to live it to the fullest. Be bold! Be courageous! I am right there with you every second.

Don't let fear or worry get in your way. They are robbers. They rob you of the exciting and joyful life that I have planned for you. Don't worry about what might go wrong, or what your friends might say. Trust Me enough to face problems as they come, instead of making up problems to worry about. Whenever you start to feel afraid, remember that I am holding your hand. Nothing can separate you from My Presence!

HEBREWS 12:2

"I am the Lord
your God. I am
HOLDING your
right hand.
And I tell you,
'Don't be afraid.
I will **HELP** you.'"

—Isaiah 41:13 (ICB)

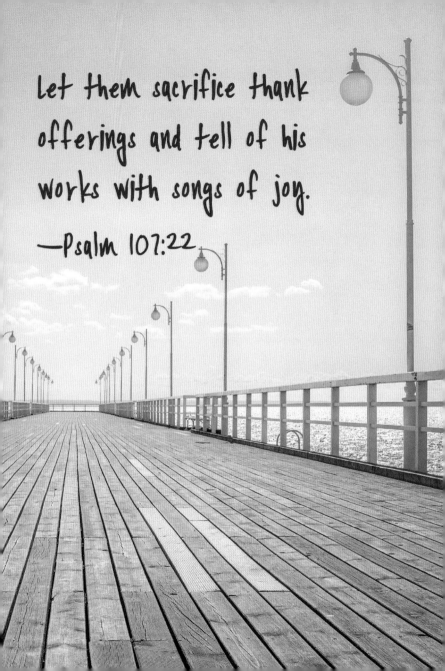

Let them sacrifice thank offerings and tell of his works with songs of joy.

—Psalm 107:22

FLIPPING THE SWITCH

When you thank Me for the difficult things in your life, suddenly they are no longer as difficult. How this works is a mystery.

But if you will give Me thanks—even for the things that make you sad or upset—then I will give you Joy. And you can have that Joy no matter what is happening.

For those who don't know Me well, thanking Me for heartaches and hardships seems impossible—even silly. But if you step out in faith and thank Me, you will be blessed. You may still be in the same yucky situation, but it will be as if someone flipped on the light switch in a dark room. You'll see things in the Light of My Presence—from *My* point of view—and realize that you aren't alone. My Presence will make your troubles not so troublesome.

EPHESIANS 5:20; PSALM 89:15

Give THANKS

to the LORD,

for he is good;

his love

ENDURES

forever.

—PSALM 118:1

NEVER STOP PRAYING

ever stop praying. How is that even possible? Try thanking Me for every blessing you encounter in your day. Not just your meals, or when you aced your test—but when you wake up, when you finish a class, when you get to see your friends, even when you face the "hidden blessings" of troubles or challenges.

If you are serious about learning to pray at all times, then thank Me in every situation. Don't get hung up on saying the "right" words—prayer doesn't have to be fancy or formal. Just say, "Thank You" and mean it. This is a great starting point for all your other prayers too.

When you're caught up in thanking Me, you won't have time for worrying or complaining. This will make you much happier. You will be training your mind to keep talking with Me. And that's really what "never stop praying" is all about.

JAMES 4:8; ROMANS 15:13

Always be JOYFUL.

Never stop PRAYING.

Be THANKFUL in

all circumstances.

—1 Thessalonians 5:16–18 (nlt)

NEVER GIVE UP!

I am always with you and for you. I am your biggest fan. When you decide to do something that fits My plans for you, nothing in heaven or on earth can stop you. You may face some problems along the way to your goal—that is part of living in an imperfect world. But never give up! With My help, you can conquer any problem.

But don't just rush headlong toward your goal, trying to make things happen when you want them to. First, come to Me. Ask Me to guide you every step of the way, minute by minute. Let Me set the pace. Sometimes I may ask you to wait, or to slow down, or even to stop for a while. But remember, My timing is perfect. Trust Me and enjoy sharing the journey with Me.

ROMANS 8:31; PSALM 46:1–3; LUKE 1:37

NOTHING

is

IMPOSSIBLE

for God!

—LUKE 1:37 (CEV)

THE BEST LIFE

People search for life in all kinds of ways. They spend their time on fun and pleasures. They buy more stuff. They do whatever it takes to be popular, rich, or famous. They chase after things that won't even matter in a few years—and certainly not in eternity.

Meanwhile, I am waiting. Look for *Me*. I am Life! To those who seek Me, I give abundant Life. That means I pour Myself into you—My Joy, My Presence, My Love. I fill you with My purpose and work in this world through you. Not only will your life make a difference on this earth, but also you will build up treasures in heaven. Come to Me, and I will give you the very best life.

MATTHEW 11:28–29;

1 PETER 1:8–9; MATTHEW 6:19

JESUS said to her,

"I am the resurrection

and the life. He who

BELIEVES in me will live,

even though he dies."

—John 11:25

SHHH . . . BE STILL

I come to you when you are still and quiet. It is then that you can hear Me speaking to your heart.

Don't be discouraged if it is hard to find a quiet time and place. This world likes everything to be loud and fast. Try slipping out into the backyard and letting the sounds of My creation draw you to Me. Shut the door to your room, and close out the world for a while. Turn off the music, and tune in to Me.

My eyes are always on the lookout for a heart that is seeking Me. And that person is so very precious to Me. I know when you are trying to find Me, and My heart is blessed by your efforts.

ZECHARIAH 2:13; 2 CHRONICLES 16:9;
PSALM 23:3

He MAKES me

to lie down in

green pastures;

He LEADS me

beside the still waters.

—Psalm 23:2 (nkjv)

therefore, there is now
no condemnation for those
who are in Christ Jesus.

—Romans 8:1

YOUR GREATEST PROTECTION

If you want to have a thankful heart, you must work to protect it. Remember that you live in a fallen world, full of sin. Both blessings and sorrows are all around you, and they are mixed up together. Work to keep your heart and mind focused on the good things.

Too many of My children choose to focus on the hard times and the trouble. They walk through a day filled with beauty and brightness, and they see only the gray of sorrow and sin. They forget to look for My blessings, and darkness fills their minds.

Thankfulness is your greatest protection against that darkness. When your heart is thankful, you know that the Light of My Presence is shining on you. And you can walk through even the grayest day with Joy in your heart.

PSALM 118:24

I will **OFFER**

you a sacrifice of

THANKSGIVING,

and call on the

name of the Lord.

—Psalm 116:17 (nlt)

THE LANGUAGE
OF HEAVEN

When you live your life praising and thanking Me for the blessings I give you each day, your life becomes filled with miracles. It is as if a blindfold has been removed from your eyes. With your eyes wide open, you see more and more of My glorious riches. So let your thankfulness sing out My praises!

A thankful heart keeps you focused on Me and what I am doing in your life. Instead of trying to be in control, you relax and make Me the Center of your life. This is the way I created you to live, and it is a way of Joy.

Your joyful praises are the language of heaven—and the true language of your heart.

PSALM 100:4 (ICB); COLOSSIANS 3:15;
REVELATION 19:3–6; PSALM 100:5

IMMEDIATELY,

something that looked

like fish scales fell from

Saul's eyes. He was able to

SEE again! Then Saul got

up and was baptized.

—Acts 9:18

DON'T LOOK
AT THE WAVES

Problems are all around you, like the waves in the ocean. But don't look at the waves. Look at Me, and I will keep you safe. If you look only at the waves—at the problems—you will sink in an ocean of worry and fear. Don't be afraid. Simply call out, "Help me, Jesus!" and I will lift you up—just as I did Peter.

I know that you sometimes worry about what's ahead. The future can be frightening—like gigantic waves just waiting to crash down on you. Trust in Me. I already know the future. By the time those gigantic waves get to you, I will have shrunk them down to a size you can face. And I am always beside you, helping you. The closer you are to Me, the safer you will be.

HEBREWS 12:2; PHILIPPIANS 4:7

And Peter left the boat

and WALKED on the water

to Jesus. But when Peter

saw the wind and the

waves, he BECAME afraid

and began to sink. He

shouted, "Lord, save me!"

—Matthew 14:29–30 (icb)

LISTEN FOR MY VOICE

There are lots of voices out there trying to get your attention. Friends, television—and yes, even the devil. They all try to tell you what is important and how you should act. And often, they all say something different. If you listen to all those voices, you will end up running in circles and getting nowhere—like a puppy chasing its tail!

Learn to listen for *My* voice. Learn to tell My voice apart from all the others. How is that possible? *Pray.* Ask My Spirit to help you hear My voice above all the others. Listen closely to what I have to say, and then follow Me wherever I lead.

EPHESIANS 4:1–6

"His sheep

FOLLOW

him because they

KNOW his voice."

—John 10:4

HINTS OF HEAVEN

Did you know that you can get a glimpse of heaven right now, here on earth? When you walk along your life-path with Me, you are already experiencing the most important part of heaven—nearness to Me. And all throughout your day, you can find hints of heaven along your pathway.

The morning sunlight that opens your eyes can remind you that in heaven there is no darkness; there is only the Light of My Presence. The birds teach you how to sing My praises—loud and strong and filled with joy. The flowers, the trees, and the skies can all give you glimpses of the beauty that is waiting for you in heaven.

As you walk through your day today, keep your eyes and ears fully open. Hints of heaven are all around you!

1 CORINTHIANS 15:20–23

We have this HOPE

as an anchor

for the soul,

firm and SECURE.

It enters the inner

sanctuary behind

the curtain.

—Hebrews 6:19

Blessed are those who have learned to acclaim you, who walk in the light of your presence, O Lord.

—Psalm 89:15

ALWAYS AND PERFECTLY

There is nothing—and no one—in this world that is perfect. Things break, friends let you down, and even your parents lose their cool sometimes.

Only I am perfect. And I love you perfectly—*always*. Let your body, mind, and spirit relax in that fact. Be awed by the vastness of My Love for you. It is wider than any continent, longer than any road, higher than any mountain, and deeper than any ocean. This vast Love is yours—forever!

The best possible response to My Love is thankfulness. Thank Me for loving you, for being your Savior, and for taking care of you. Then just watch to see how much I bless you.

1 Peter 5:7; Ephesians 3:16–19;
Psalm 107:22

Let them give

THANKS

to the LORD for

his unfailing love and

his WONDERFUL

deeds for men.

—PSALM 107:21

IN THE RIGHT DIRECTION

When you learn to ride a bike, you quickly learn to keep your eyes on where you want the bike to go. If you look away, then you're likely to go off in the wrong direction—and crash into a ditch or a tree! Wherever your eyes go, your bike soon follows.

Your thoughts are much the same. Keep your thoughts focused on Me and My will for you. People and situations change all the time. And the world whirls around like the scenery flying past a car window. If you focus too long on the world, you will get dizzy and confused. But I never change. Keep your thoughts on Me, and I will keep you moving in the right direction.

PSALM 102:27

We must keep our

EYES on Jesus,

who leads us and

makes our FAITH

complete.

—Hebrews 12:2 (cev)

THE BEST SECURITY SYSTEM EVER

I am your Strength and your Shield. Long before you get out of bed each morning, I am there, preparing and planning your day. Instead of wondering what will happen and worrying about how you will handle it, talk to Me about it. I've already got it all figured out. If you ask for My help, My Strength will flow freely into you. You will be strong enough to face whatever comes.

If you start to feel afraid, remember that I am your Shield. I'm not just a piece of cold metal—I am alive, always on the alert. I watch over you every minute, protecting you from both known and unknown dangers. I never sleep; I never take a break; I never get distracted.

Trust yourself to My Strength and My Shield—I am the best security system you'll ever find!

MATTHEW 6:34; PSALM 56:3–4;
GENESIS 28:15

The LORD is

my STRENGTH

and shield. I

TRUST him,

and he HELPS me.

—PSALM 28:7 (ICB)

I MAKE YOU COMPLETE

This world moves so fast—and not just cars, jet planes, and rocket ships. People and events move fast. *You're* expected to move fast. There are so many things you're supposed to do, so many places to go, so many people demanding your attention. Like riding too long on a merry-go-round, it can make you dizzy and leave you feeling empty inside.

When everything is spinning too fast, come to Me. I will stop the spinning.

The world says it can make you whole and complete—just *do* this, or *be* that. But the world only takes; it doesn't give back. Only I can make you whole. I can fill up the emptiness with My Love, Joy, and Peace. You will be complete—and then you can help others find Me too.

1 JOHN 4:12

But the

fruit of the

SPIRIT is love,

joy, peace, patience,

kindness, goodness,

FAITHFULNESS,

gentleness and

self-control.

—GALATIANS 5:22–23

CELEBRATE THE GIFT

I am eternal. Forever. When I speak, it is from the depths of eternity. Before the world was formed, I AM! And when this world is gone, I will still be the same.

I have come to live inside your heart. I am Christ in you. I, your Lord and Savior, am alive within you! Learn to tune in to My living Presence by seeking Me in quietness.

As you celebrate the wonder of My birth in Bethlehem, remember to celebrate also *your* birth into eternal life. This amazing gift was My purpose for coming into your world. Enjoy My gift with a humble, thankful heart. Take time to explore how huge My Love for you really is. And let My Peace rule in your heart, because you know how much I love you.

COLOSSIANS 1:27; COLOSSIANS 3:15

Before the mountains

were **BORN**, before you

gave birth to the earth

and the world, from

BEGINNING to end,

you are God.

—Psalm 90:2 (NLT)

"Sacrifice thank offerings to God, fulfill your vows to the Most High."

—Psalm 50:14